THE MAN WAS A STRANGER

THE MAN WAS A STRANGER

POONAM SINGH

Copyright © Poonam Singh
All Rights Reserved.

This book has been self-published with all reasonable efforts taken to make the material error-free by the author. No part of this book shall be used, reproduced in any manner whatsoever without written permission from the author, except in the case of brief quotations embodied in critical articles and reviews.

The Author of this book is solely responsible and liable for its content including but not limited to the views, representations, descriptions, statements, information, opinions and references ["Content"]. The Content of this book shall not constitute or be construed or deemed to reflect the opinion or expression of the Publisher or Editor. Neither the Publisher nor Editor endorse or approve the Content of this book or guarantee the reliability, accuracy or completeness of the Content published herein and do not make any representations or warranties of any kind, express or implied, including but not limited to the implied warranties of merchantability, fitness for a particular purpose. The Publisher and Editor shall not be liable whatsoever for any errors, omissions, whether such errors or omissions result from negligence, accident, or any other cause or claims for loss or damages of any kind, including without limitation, indirect or consequential loss or damage arising out of use, inability to use, or about the reliability, accuracy or sufficiency of the information contained in this book.

Made with ♥ on the Notion Press Platform
www.notionpress.com

This book is related to a stranger. On which I have composed this story. The name of that person is Abhimanyu Pandit (Abu). Looks innocent. The one above has blessed with excellent eyes and style.

That person behaves very politely with a stranger. Knowingly or unknowingly a meeting happened. It is a beautiful coincidence that friendship has also started. We spent some moments together as friends. The medium of this story is also some moments spent together there. That moment was the most beautiful moment of my life. Met good people and made good friendships. For all this, I thank that stranger from the bottom of my heart. I will pray to God that even after the completion of this story, this friendship should remain safe.

Enter Caption

Contents

Foreword

This story is written in Hindi language. Mainly in this story, the emotion of love has been displayed. Through which love has been presented in a different way. Mainly falling in love or keeping yourself a villain in love. These are two different things. It has also been shown in the love of God, that love is not one sided. Maybe it is the love story of Maa Sita and Shri Ram or the story of Shiva and Parvati or the love story of Krishna and Radha. One thing was common in all of them.It was a two sided unbreakable love. Love doesn't mean just being close. That is, the decrease of love due to the increase of distance, love cannot happen, this is Kalyug. The importance of love is less than feelings, you are more important than selfishness.

Preface

Through this book, from the meeting of a stranger to the journey of friendship, it has been mentioned in front of all of you.

This story is particularly close to my heart. In this book I have tried to present that strange set of meeting strangers. Surely you will see a glimpse of love in it, but there is a suggestion that you must know before reading this book, "Every gaze that rises towards you with love is never love".

Acknowledgements

When you read this book, I hope you will be able to understand an important difference. If you can understand the difference between innocence and maturity, you will be able to better understand the difference between love, deep friendship, friend and only friend. Apart from parents, some relations are very important in our life. It is very important to keep it safe.

Lastly, I pray for all of you that all of you are successful in your every relationship.

Prologue

I would mainly like to thank that moment. The moment I met "a stranger". That's when I started this story. And then I am also thankful to all those who spent their valuable time with me to bring this story to life. As a result of which, This story has come to an end.Helped make my journey from strangers to family more beautiful. These people have played an important role, so I would like to include the names of others.

1. Abhimanyu
2. Abhishek
3. Harshita
4 . Sejal
5 . Abhishek Jaggi
6 . Tripti

And the last one is "senya" that means myself are also involved in this.

I would like to thank all of you from the bottom of my heart.

About Author

I am Poonam Singh a graduate student. I am twenty years old. I belong to a small town in the Vaishali district. I have also done my education till class 12th from Jawahar Navodaya Vidyalaya (Vaishali). During her school days, she often enrolled herself in co-curricular activities. Such as Chess, Yoga, Badminton, Kho-Kho, Basketball, Handball, NCC, Scouts and Guides, Group dance, and painting arts often participated and also achieved some achievements.
Surely these achievements have no value at the educational level. But all these things play an important role in turning you into a better person. I used to compose poems often on Hindi Diwas. Just understood that the hobby of writing came from there. It is said that when you adopt loneliness, then pen and paper play well with you.

poonamsingh_8898

CHAPTER ONE

The Man Was a Stranger

1. This evening is very pleasant
This night is very drunk.
Look at the beggars of love,
There is so much water in his eyes.

A picture came to the fore
Saw that he got intoxicated.
There will be no love again,
All these hearts have to go.
But the heart got hurt and broke,
So to be scattered on the floor.
Even if someone else is added,
This mark has to remain for life.

We love someone unconditionally and he turns away
why should we love
We do loyalty and he is called unfaithful
why should we love
we break up again and can't connect
why should we love

get shattered again and don't even have patience
why should we love

Then let's not talk about love, just live its feeling, but you will think how can I tell how?

My self Poonam Singh. I am basically from Bihar. And this is the story about to live the feeling of love, you have to read this story written by me titled (the man was a stranger) This story explains the feeling of one sided love. Where it also teaches you to handle yourself in love. And sometimes falling in love too. Then will you read this story of mine, lovely story, I am sure you must be smiling while reading it.

The man was a stranger

I am very disappointed with the happiness of life.
I gave up hope, I had no shortage of people, but I had built a new home of mine. This was going on sometime in June-July.
A month where people get affected by the scorching sun. Leaving work and abode, they go out in search of rest. But this was not the case with me. My routine was a little different from others. Staying in your room all day, spending hours on the study table, then falling asleep after being fed up, but did not move from the study table until sleep engulfed your eyes, studying on the same table, painting and watching people sitting in a closed room just like that. To understand, to study psychology, it is good to do all these things.The rest of the time was spent in the dreams shown by father. Still, I don't have any complaints about it. But when I get angry even a little bit, I cry profusely. They know that I am very naive and delicate at heart. On the contrary, this world is full of deceit. That's why they come and celebrate after every scolding. And he

also explains, he knows, to his daughter and he also believes that, my daughter has yet to reach the heights of the sky. From where she will shine like the stars. But the journey till there was not easy. In this journey, some relationships will be true, some will be angels, some unfaithful will also be found.You will get more deception than people. That's why they keep reprimanding my delicate heart. And when their hearts are full, they often come to me and celebrate.

But today this story is of one sided love, isn't it? So let's hide this story in the heart. And those who settle the turmoil that has taken place on the other side of the heart. The upheaval of love and one sided love.

" Listen, this is the talk of the heart " I am just saying to you. You will not share with anyone else, will you? Yes, even if I get free time from things like my studies, yoga, painting and writing poetry, then every evening is spent in the name of the family members.But that evening was unique. In the era of online, probably people started doing offline. Perhaps, but now what to do with the distance, I too used to visit Instagram on the pretext of posting status. Now it has become like a daily habit. No matter how much busyness is there in life, she used to get a glance.

But today's evening was more special, a lot of time had passed. But I was stuck on just one Instagram profile, and probably stuck for a long time. Something was different. She was looking like some ocean waves in the eyes of the man. Like the ocean, cool as well as steady, smiling and giggling too but he was a stranger.As if such a voice is coming from the face, that like girls don't slip, I am not with you to handle. And just don't know how much time of that evening was lost to me. Perhaps a lot of time has passed while staring at a stranger, it was realized after a long time that I have spent a lot of time, just staring at a face.

I thought it would be a thought for some time and then it would go away. He handled himself with great difficulty. When this thought came, I got a suggestion, my heart used to say that you should talk but my brain kept me safe.Now it was the time when my exams were completely over. And for a long time I used to tell just like that on social media. In the free time, there was often a thought of a stranger. Till now it seemed as if in the battle of heart and mind, only the heart is allowed to win. The brain said that we celebrate happiness only after (defeat), whatever you do, you can talk.Come on, in the battle of heart and mind, the heart has made the mind. But how to talk, what to talk about, this was a big problem. Then what was it like CID scrutinized the profile of Instagram for two whole days and tried to find out something. But still could not find out whether this stranger knows how to read and write Hindi or not.But there was one thing that we both had in common. Some pictures of NCC camp, now what was it, just one arrow and two marks, it has become the same thing.

Now the plan was ready, it just had to be executed so that the matter could be done. While sitting singing a song, I messaged with great love, "Hello sir" Will you help me, I sent the message by writing this much. Then I write in another message that these NCC certificates will be useful for admission in your college. After that, I had a feeling that a reply to the message may also come. Nothing else can be said, so I don't want to shrink my heart.Because I know myself better. I really hate late replies, and none of my friends reply late to me. But I know. I never message anyone. When there are useful things, then it is also natural that the reply to the message comes immediately. But the problem here was not with those who knew. It was from a stranger. Now the stranger knew me. And neither did I know him. It was natural for the reply to come late.So my brain also made my heart understand that it is possible not to feel bad, whether the message comes late or not, which one is my own, my knower. After all, he is a stranger, isn't he? Overall, I had already understood myself mentally. And she was careful too, and even if I don't get a reply, I don't mind.But these were the figments of my mind. Whatever I thought so much, Mother, unlike whom did not reply to my message within 24 hours, I remember that I had sent the first message on May 27, 2022 only. And his reply came on the 28th. What do you think, what would have come ? nothing special the result of so much hard work was settled by just saying "Yes". But come on, this is also fine, my question was yes, no, wali. What can even a stranger do in this? Provided all this is me myself. It was being said from the very beginning because one has to console himself, isn't it?I think all these competitive exams give entrance exams. It has become their habit. To end every question in one answer, now what is their fault in this too. And it was okay too, I was not angry because I had questions. However, they were of one word only. Now the matter was equal whether the answers were found in one word or whole stories were told.

Well leave it, let these things go. I was thinking, what to talk about now, now there is no issue. How can I do friendship, should I speak directly?

And then what was it, I started investigating again like CID and then I came to know that this stranger knows Hindi very well.After a long time no face has been seen.

We were strangers in an unknown street.
But at first sight,
His picture has come to mind.

Then thought that some time should pass,
Then this picture is going to get lost in the mist.
We were strangers before,
You have to pass on the street as a stranger.
If you are forbidden only about this,
that when the heart has longed for someone,
Why are you hiding?
Have a little courage and believe
Expressing without thinking about the consequences.

2. ,And because I am in the world of thoughts, the question is also mine and the answer is also mine, so read the next lines. And here I am preparing that how should I do if I want to be friends, I don't know what to say, so I was just not doing anything in preparation.

it was a while ago,
When I saw your picture for the first time.
Seeing the innocence of the face, my heart melted.
Nano's glimpse on the fairy picture and my heart fluttered.
Now something like this happened,
Meet me at one o'clock in the day.
I started coming to this street everyday,
Seeing a glimpse, she started guarding the picture everyday like this.Although these were some confused words of mine. Which I was putting on the pages. But yes it was just the beginning of a friendship. You can see the glimpse of love, can't you? But believe me, love does not happen so quickly, it takes time for love to happen. It takes time to understand each other, seeing at a glance what you call love is only attraction. How can anyone fall in love with someone just by looking at the outer structure, I can't. God has made man so deep, that no matter how much you try to understand him, you will go on searching, time will fly

by. But a person will understand with great difficulty, now loving someone in such a way that too one sided brother will not be able to be with me.

How can anyone say that one sided love should not cause pain. I think one sided love doesn't give trouble, it gives disrespect. How can anyone say that one sided love should not cause pain. I think one sided love doesn't give trouble, it gives disrespect. Where there is only one person in your thoughts. And brother, don't know to what extent we come in that person's thoughts or not, brother, what do we know? Now imagine whether you would like to have one sided love in such a way or would love in such a way where the person in front knows that you love him and he also likes you. It is obvious that you would like to live in such a love where the person in front appreciates your love and cares for you.And I know, I think that the claimants of one sided love are the buyers of love. Neither there is anyone Meera in this Kalyug. And neither does anyone give up his life in love like Meera. This is not the love of the Copper Age. This is the love of Kalyug. Here people will be infatuated with you for a moment. And the second moment you will love someone else, now tell me, do you think this is love, dear, not so impure.But it is true that if someone is in love, then you can clearly see his jealousy and his affection for you.

His concern is visible for you. Because this is the love of Kalyug. But there is only love, isn't it?

And I cannot call this attraction a disease of love. I love to write, so it is normal for me to live in a world of thoughts. That is, it does not mean that I am not aware of the reality or I am not aware of the world of this Kalyug.

Because it was very clear in my head that I am not in love and I don't even want to be in love right now. Because in order to be loved, knowing someone better and including someone in your time, including yourself in his habits, the beginning of love is something like this. And right now time does not allow itself to indulge in someone's habits.But how long will this complaint last, how long will you let yourself go away from yourself. The distance had increased for so many days. But still the upheaval in the heart was not ending. I thought that if the distance increases more, then maybe those memories and pictures will disappear from the eyes. These thoughts often come to mind. Every evening my time is wasted. This too will reduce, or will end, this thought will also go out of my mind.

But do you know that sometimes the things that go on in your heart and mind and if it takes a lot of your time, then it is better that the thought is for whom. You share with him once because he is the sharer of that thought. The person who comes in your thoughts is also responsible.

What was it then, I had decided. Let's talk now, after all, what is the harm in friendship. Now boys or girls extend the hand of friendship, all are equal. At least these everyday thoughts will not bother you. Because it was a bit difficult, I was a bit scared to ask a stranger for a number just like that, there was a bit of hesitation. But in this online era, love and friendship are all the same.Had to make sure Now till when the account remains or not, how many times have I changed the account. And the people who are connected on WhatsApp, may not talk to them. There is a feeling of their presence.

After thinking all this, I shamelessly demanded the number this time. Now if you get it, then you have heard that "Hum aapke hai kaun?"You know . I got the number immediately without any question without any fuss, but the problem was that, I was thinking, how can someone just give his number without knowing anything without asking anything. And this question came from the depths of my mind, I started thinking whether I have been given a wrong number, I asked that stranger whether your number is correct or not. Is this a professional number or not, I was asking just like that, means you just gave it without asking any question, that too immediately there was a slight hesitation.

But that stranger had a personal number. Then I took the number yes I didn't say directly that I want your number I had picketed the matter a bit I said you will add us on whatsapp what is that, I don't always use Instagram. it might as well be deleted.Yes, it is also true that, don't know how many times I have created a new profile of my Instagram. What is it now that I do not know anything about technology, I am unable to do anything. Sometimes I do something like this. And if something like this clicked, then everything went in the water, at least the number remained so that it could connect with friends again.

But what is the use of taking the number, I don't even know what I will do.But I didn't have any problem with it. Because I was also a stranger. What to talk to a stranger in front of that stranger. Till then everything was fine. But one day suddenly a question came from the stranger and what was the question? Will you meet our friends? I was not interesting on the inside. Because I knew. The things that normally happen in the group will be just time pass.There were many questions in the mind, don't know what kind of people will be there in the group. Must be criticizing each other. Naturally it was possible. In the group of friends, there is talk only on condemnation. Or there is a strong subject. On which people give their views. Because this was not the second group.

Probably the first group. But still I agreed thinking that

all are educated people. Will get to learn something. Some seniors share their things, some are important for our subject so keep knowing. Keep getting some knowledge, and I can always gain knowledge. So I don't see any harm in not joining that group. But still, before joining, I convince myself and my brain that, after all, group fun is fun. Don't let it take you to heart.And that's how it started. Another unique story from a stranger of mine.And that's how I come. In a new family where I join (Star family) where people are good. From whom you can learn a lot. And I got a chance to know that stranger i.e. (Abu) aka Abhimanyu from close quarters as well as so many more characters through which I can understand his personality. Also, all were much older than me. So I will continue to feel the world. This is a good opportunity to know their experiences.I had this much apprehension that after my arrival a lot has been mentioned about me in this group. Don't know what kind of reflection has already been made. Don't know how I will establish my reflection because my own characters are so different don't ask. It was very difficult to understand. Consider them like family or keep them in the circle of a friend. But I decided that I would keep them within the confines of one family. because the name of this group was star family. probably like a family, so I decided that I would also keep them in the circle of family.

And my conversations started with everyone. Everyone was lovely with an affinity. Everyone welcomed me well but because I thought of keeping them in a family circle, I preferred to open myself more. And I started living like I live at home. Carefree, cool, just let me speak whatever comes to my heart. There is a little hesitation, because whether it is there or not, it just seems like our own.

Conversing in reality on the basis of guess can beat me somewhere.

The first day passed well, talked to everyone. Got to know everyone a little and liked everyone. There will be a group of about seven people. An Abhishek whom we will address as Bade Bhaiya, an Abhimanyu who is a stranger to me and probably still is. One Abhishek Jaggi. Gave Parag and Sejal, Gave Tripti and Harshu Gave Vaishali and Muskaan. And all the people were in the city, I got acquainted with only these many.

But maybe luck is not that good, on the very first day I felt as if someone had killed me even after being speechless. There was a person who probably did not like my presence or he got angry because of my talking too much.

This is Abhishek Bhaiya who does not like to talk much. And maybe the speed of my message was a bit too fast, yes because I was curious. Where I have gone, there was curiosity to know the people there. Otherwise, so many messages told us that I am talkative, but where are I when I see strangers along with my own. He had some questions from us and after that he separated himself from that group, it was like a mockery. Which hurt me a little on the first meeting itself.And I decided to say goodbye from there and left that group. If it was not possible to know everyone so closely in one day. This uprooted feeling probably gave me some trouble. But the talk ended and then everyone got back together.Days passed and things started happening. But I am not fit yet. The issue was that even after coming close to the person whom I wanted to know, I could not get to know him but I have started getting to know his close friend better, this is a very strange thing but it is true. There was no harm in knowing his close ones. But Malal was definitely said in the heart that, the person who has to know better. Nothing is known about that person except his name. But somewhere in my heart, I had definitely thought that I don't want to send any message anymore.Not in front, but whenever there are mutual talks between those people, then I definitely have a doubt about it. Things are bad or things are good, I don't know but these things happen. I doubt it.

3. It was a pleasant evening, that moment was fun.
When that person came in front of me.
The Aaya of this universe had descended on my face.

Humility is my decoration, I think with modesty.
If the eyes bow down in front of you then it is a shame.
There is no trust of love, there is no fever of love.
Jashn e Hayat is my destiny by staying away from love.

This was the day when the video call happened for the first time. I used to think but then thought, what is the use, there is no time to think so much, let's sit and dress up for someone. Smiling is my style. He smiles even when he is angry. Smiles even in hatred. Smiles even in love. Smiles even in modesty. Otherwise, they remain silent. But this time was very strange.The only complaint was that we don't know each other yet, it is enough to know, but we don't recognize each other yet. I understand people find some people like this. Then some people become special. I was not in love I said about friendship.

How much heart hurts, doesn't it, when someone makes you wait flawlessly. Yes, I am also sad. I have waited too. There were some questions which had to be answered. But that person is a mushroom. My questions were less, maybe he asked some more questions without getting answers, now I am not feeling at peace. He says that he is broken in love, no one cares for his love, what to do. Where is she, maybe there is some deficiency, she doesn't want me in me with the desire that I want.Hearing this, I was a little worried that why should anyone forbid this person, there is neither any shortcoming nor any fault. Then why should anyone deny, but I am not surprised to know this. I know that if a girl's heart falls on a poor person, then that person is the prince of her dreams for that girl. And if the girl does not like any prince, then he hardly matters in her life. There are other things besides this money and status. Which girls want to see in their favorite shoes.The preference of each girls is determined by her individually. That girl might not want any partner right now or maybe she is not getting the kind of partner she wants or the same personal behavior in this person. These were our guesses. Only God knows the reality.This question stuck in my mind as if I don't listen to the whole story, I don't know what is the reality, till then I will not be at peace. Don't know how many times I must have asked that person for some time for himself, but maybe he is busy in his own world. I don't have any complaint about this but the question which is in my mind, it is necessary to sleep, it is taking my time, it is troubling me. There were already so many complications. Now one day someone asked in the group just like that. Senya do you like Abu. I said yes, I like it. I know everyone must have claimed liking as a feeling of love.

If there is no one, I have also allowed this series to continue like this. After all, there should have been some subject. That which can be talked about, debated, drawn upon and enjoyed, or, perhaps for a while, the reason that people are attached to each other. However, being pranked gets me nothing but trouble. This is the reason why I neither criticize nor allow anyone to do so. The people behind me are free citizens to do what they want. I never judge anyone.I know this is their way of talking. There is nothing inappropriate in this, it is just a little contrary to my methods. To live in a group, one has to ignore such activities.As I began to differ with that stranger, I began to understand that he was really very different from me. My ways are very different. There is a strange hesitation, these relationships consider me mindless because of my ignorance. But what should I do, I am also helpless, I also have two ways, the first one is to maintain friendship from the heart. In which my foolishness and my childish actions are also included. And the second is to maintain friendship like a smart girl, as we maintain other relationships which we call friendship.Friendship in name only for work. Because I don't have any such purpose or any such special work which can be completed by someone other than me, then I cannot have a work relationship with anyone here, it would be appropriate that I separate myself from this group.But the people were not bad. There was no point in staying away from him. Then I learned from the river that there are obstacles in the way but still it keeps on flowing merging in its speed. Just thinking this made up my mind to stay there. I'm weird, I know it. I don't like any abusive word and I don't want people around me to use such words whether its language is English or Hindi or whatever. I started ignoring the abusive words used in hymns, laughter and jokes.

We have two choices on every path. The first is what we want, the way we want and the second is what our branch relatives and relatives want. Or an option also comes that your thoughts match with friends and relatives.

Believe me, this third option is a very strange option, your close ones are happy and you are also satisfied with this option.But what about those whose views do not match with those of their relatives? Personally, if my opinion is taken on this subject, I would say that a person's personality is his identity, so there is no need to change it till then. until they feel themselves. But it is said that "change is the rule of the world".But this does not mean at all that we should misunderstand the people around us, misunderstand their ideologies, our intelligence is only in this. That we should not accept the things which we find unacceptable by being with them, but by being with them.And there I have met very nice people. Yes, it may be that I am lucky that I have met so many lovely people with whom I started talking very well on my first meeting. I had already got to know Abu a little, but here I found so many more lovely people which I might not have even imagined.Abhishek Bhaiya was a bit strict in the first meeting but in reality he is a soft hearted person. You care a lot for the people close to you. Surely he is a very good person at heart. And his girlfriend, his personality is also very calm. I will pray to God that both of them remain safe forever, I have seen many people, good as well as bad, that's why I was not surprised to meet good people, but for the first time, I was giving importance to strangers after your family.

Shejal Rai is also a different kind of woman. I know a very caring girl. Takes care of you. Knowingly or unknowingly, I have learned a lot from him. I have come in this group, but I am not crazy about anyone's love, I wanted to know a person a little closer. How can anyone love anyone from whose gross? The beginning of love happens when we start liking someone's personality, we start getting used to someone's absence, we feel his absence due to someone's absence. I am very worried, this is my habit too.Abu is worried about some issue, maybe he is worried about someone and now I have also become a part of this problem. I just want to know the whole thing, after all, what is the issue and if I can help, then it is okay, otherwise it will be assumed that there is no solution to some issue. But after telling the incomplete thing, I don't know why this person does not tell the whole thing, I am getting worried, maybe thinking of someone else's issue. But these people have given a different name to my problem.

Oops, how can I explain that I am not bothered by one sided love. I can't even have one-sided love.

Sejal di called today. They think I am troubled by the expectation of one-sided love. By the way, it was good to see the concern of Sejal and Abu. But what did I do, in order to solve my problem, I made Sejal Di angry. I just wanted to tell the whole story or the truth, but Di got very angry with Abu. Uff man, how can I be so mad.

What a strange thing, isn't it? These people had come to make me carefree. And I entangled the quarrel between these two and I could not even convince Sejal Di, but it was not my fault either. It was a small thing, Abu should have told it himself, even if he called, it was a conference call and in the conversation, I came to know that this saree is a lie, a fabricated story. Don't worry about me. And thinking here, I told Sejal Di. I know I am stupid but surely it was not my fault I cannot argue with anyone, nor can I agree with anyone. I think I did the best I could. And now I am leaving fere.

Today I came back after a long time. Perhaps it is also the birthday of Harshita di. This is probably someone's first birthday after my arrival, that's why I have tried to make it a little funny, my condition is very serious at the moment but still, I had already made a promise, now I cannot back down. Good day everyone had a lot of fun

today and probably smiled a lot at my stupidity, let's go well.
Happy to see these people are probably lucky. WhomI introduced you in childhood because I have never given time to friendship till now and I have only a few months. In which I can know more about these people and can recognize them.
Today is also the birthday of Abhishek Jaggi. But all are very busy with their exams and some are busy with their jobs. I am also busy enough. Uff yaara, but on this day, he will not like it if someone does partiality knowingly or unknowingly, and how much time will it take me to draw a picture? I will make a maximum of 15 minutes at any time.
I know anyway. I am a guest for a few days. People may smile or become happy because of me. I have no loss in this. My attempt was just to know the personality of a person. But something else happened here, it is said that whatever happens is for the good. No one knows what I stole from this group. As much time as I have given to this group.I have saved your future maximum time from that. I am very lucky that God has put me in contact with such good people, but I think now is the time to keep some distance. Perhaps those people have already known as much as they wanted to know about me, there is no point in knowing and the rest will be known in the future without telling, my effort will be here only.

@its_dr.abhi

Some Quotes & Poetry

© Love or edge
To go from this street to that street, the traveler must cover the distance to reach the destination.

©My dear luck
Someone makes me cry so much.
Like someone is broken and the other one makes it worse.

©Why are you so sad, it seems that someone close is gone.
The middle of keeping an oath by giving has been left in the middle.

This is the custom of the world.
One moment someone has to come.
One moment someone has to go.
Then why there's shedding tears about this situation?

©If something has happened,
Please say to me. "naaa" ......
Don't be so silent.
I have done something wrong.
Then punish me. " Naaaa"...
Don't sit angrily by stealing your eyes from me like this.
If you want to complain to me then do it "naa" ...
At least talk to me on this pretext. "Naaaaa"...
Why have you sat so upset, please
Forgive me for the last time. "Naaa"...

©Last time I was in love
I was in a trap which is laid by a man
I was unaware of everything.
I was so madly in love.

Then there was a change in my life
Then I took care of myself.
I had a hard time to seducing myself.
And then I forgot him.

©How precious are some relationships?
Those relationships do not have a name.
But there is a pleasant experience in a relationship.
Ishq and love don't have a name but there is a lovely feeling.
Even in the life of the part round
That moment in waiting for.
Yes, a relationship that is anonymous.

9 798889 861119

Printed by Libri Plureos GmbH in Hamburg, Germany